before the bloom
poems

by lael cassidy

*Dedicated with love to
Evan, Martin, Hannah, and Suzie,
who helped me trust the muse, and with
gratitude to the people who stood by me
when tragedy asked so much.*

Table of Contents

no body

I'm nobody because he is nobody.
He has no body and mine was his.
I am a play thrown away,
a new edition with nothing in it.
Nothing written but one line.
I am afterglow, gone. Smoke after
fireworks and no new day begun.
It takes a century to be someone.
Clear skies to grow again.
No way to do it without sun.
I'm the gray day where
you can't tell the difference between
sky and sea and cloud and anything
you might be wearing.
I am nothing but the light pouring
in your windows and into your eyes.
There and there. That's me.

Over the Shoulder

It's in my throat, the edges of it,
the electric channel, the fiery lines
that stretch on a diagonal from left
to right and rising in the air.

Death might make you notice it.
It's not nothing. It's a something that
can grab you and take you somewhere else.
Some of us live by the crack, pressing our
ears against it to hear it, not caring how
hot it is. It's not as if we choose this
real estate.

It's a given, like the parents
to whom you're born.
No one polices this lottery for fairness.
I've pretended to be normal for a while now.
Most people don't see the portal over my
shoulder, dipping its edges into
my neck.

Andromeda

Today he won't drive off in his silent
black car wearing soccer shorts and carrying
a trunk full of frisbees and pylons to play
ultimate with the other forty-something dads.
He won't race across the field, flapping his
lanky arms as though he might fly, then come home
winded, smiling, and ready to play computer
games while I heat up black bean soup and serve
him at the table that looks out over the giant
green trees we planted as saplings.
I wonder what the kids would do if they lost
me, noting the worn second-hand chair at the
desk where I used to see the back of his head
every night. There's enough money for them to
go to college, especially if they sell the house,
and there's some family to care for them,
though not mine. The stereo plays his music
as I deal with the closet. It hums darkness as
though possessed, louder as I approach its
sliding door. His narrow-waisted corduroys are
like eggs thrown at the house. You said
"No dying," I say to him—"what a funny joke."
I'm tied to a rock that lives in the void.
I pray the tide doesn't swallow me whole.

Sea

Sometimes the water is cobalt blue
with fathomless quiet, other times it is
pounded into metal, and run over with lines,
suggestive of senseless divisions and
boundaries, even mistakes.

Shadows that seem to have no basis
are replaced with bright reflections of clouds.
Sealions surface but turn out to be birds
who ducked down and, now that they've
fed, fly off. The sea, barely weighted,
floats as apparition, scarcely an attempt at
realism.

It is difficult to witness the uninterrupted
lightness of it, the furiously changing canvas,
and yes, I see the wink and nudge as I,
always too serious, gasp, terrified to witness
artist at work and me the tiniest smudge
in the painting.

Squish

The place on my arm
had magical powers.
She put her small hand
on it and squeezed
the flesh, felt
the bounce in her
fingers, the right
amount of squish.
Our bodies curved into
each other at night,
and in the morning they still fit.
I have never belonged anywhere
as much as to her,
so fierce is her hold on me.

flowers weep

flowers weep
is in the morning rain

it takes grief to leave the seed,
surrender to explode,
release to wilt,
and go to ground

the signs are everywhere
the sea cries for freedom
the mountain demands a stop
the sun burns to move

it's all the same story,
the exact same one,
this pain the same pain
a flower feels before
the bloom

Courtship

A suitor arrives in 90's hippie uniform:
army jacket with a yellow tank top under
it, leather sandals exposing hairy feet.

Dimples are carved deep in his cheeks,
and he's flushed, as though he's just
confided in me.

His dark curly hair sets off the
blue in his eyes, which, magnified by his
round glasses and the moon, glow
impossibly bright.

On the spot, he makes
up a song about my eyes.

While Cobain is "stupid and contagious,"
he sings soulfully of raven.

He is a misfit, a picnic in a world of dive bars.

He leaves a box on my doorstep full
of cherry blossoms, buoyant and pink.
They pour out, billow to the floor.

I marry him.

salt & soap

I measure words in teaspoons and cups,

often adding too much salt.

Lately I don't get the rise.

The muffins stick.

Some of the ingredients have turned foul.

There's confusion about the recipe.

The sweet turns out savory.

Honey stings.

The washing up, though necessary,

imparts soap.

Cardamom, cinnamon,

even clove won't mask it.

morning air

cloud cover
the metal of the water
the sea lions barking on the beach
the bird song, a call and response,
the placid sea
the sense of waiting
a heron's dinosaur voice
speaking a solemn bird-word

the trees stand, unperturbed,
but my children, grown, are cast
on the wind like seeds,
a seagull cries and the trilling
rolls on and on like a train
moving even if the sound doesn't
the sea lion barks again

i am that child again
whose parents never came home

here comes that train again,
like pain, already it moves
into the distance
and the wet air surrounds
with the song of its own
like a lover touching on my skin
with no intent to abandon
because there's no way it can

already i am the H, the 2, the O
it moves through me
and there's that train again,
like rain, already it moves
into the distance

Lost

Today she'll walk home from school in
the red hoodie she's worn for two years,
the one with holes in the pockets, and she'll
roll wet strands of her hair in her mouth.
Then she'll take some Lays and a soda
and sit in the gray glow of the Nintendo
until I get home and sit on the edge of
her bed and pry out words from her about how
she feels and what she will be willing to
eat for dinner before I go to the kitchen
to assemble it. She's been surfing the internet.
Scientists say we only have twenty years
before there's no turning back, she says, her flute
in its case like a life discarded, and the
holes in her sweatpants showing her bony knees
like seashells cast off by the sea.
I set for one and ask her to eat, and
she deposits herself at the table, then jumps up.
This time I'll wait on you, she smiles, and she
goes in the kitchen to get me a plate and fork.
We are sworn into service like knights,
patrolling the ramparts, and we wait,
bows in hand, but the battle is lost,
the King buried in the ground.

Parking Ticket Letters

October 17

To whom it may concern,

Enclosed you will find payment for ticket #759392 dated
September 5 which I found on my car having parked off
Commercial Street for longer than the 2-hour time limit
allowed. I had no idea it would take me so long to walk
through downtown Provincetown. It's been many years
since I've been here and so much has changed. I was
remembering hours of backgammon with my eight-year-
old son, his hair badly cut so he was often mistaken for a
girl, his blue windbreaker, his eyes still loving. He still
thought I had something to teach him maybe beyond the
wonders of backgammon, some wisdom from the male
lineage, he looked to me, and I could feel it. We rented a
place on the bay and the rhythm of the tide coming in and
out soothed something in me, the same thing the gin was
trying to do, a softening of the light, a cup full/cup empty
way to measure the day, the surface of the sea a way of
hiding all the debris underneath. The dead crab, piece of
rope, the anchor for the dingy, the way the raft we put out
there for the kids to swim to rose up, celebratory when the
tide was high, then seemed to deflate and crash, a failure
when the tide withdrew.

Sincerely,

Malcolm Fields

October 18

To whom it may concern,

I sent payment earlier for ticket#759392 received on
September 5 this year. If you haven't already, please
don't cash the check as my account no longer has
enough funds. I have recently suffered from a loss
of income that was unexpected and would like to
avoid the fee for the overdraft. I should be able to
come in directly to pay the bill within a week, and
I feel the need to return to the Cape as soon as
possible. I have been remembering now not just
the daily changes of the tide going in and out,
different each day by about an hour, marking the
moon time zone, the moon in its own rate of speed
not caring what might happen here as it pulls and
pushes, but I recall the very high tides, the ones that
suddenly grew nearly catastrophic, each wave encroaching
gradually like pancake batter spreading on a hot pan,
even sizzling at its edges with intensity, with the surge
finally pressing in on us, the waves lapping the deck,
pouring ponds on chairs and tables, snatching pillows,
hats, and sandals, and stuffing them into its endless fluid
mouth. It seems I've been trying to avoid high tide all my
life, and it's almost a relief that it's finally rolled in.

Sincerely,
Malcolm Fields

Migrant

I have walked thousands of miles in flesh,
in tiny finger-sized steps, the small but
deep movements of my hands,
navigated the lands of backs,
legs, arms, and bellies, have dived deep
 into necks, jaws, and feet, listening, pushing,
weighting the tissue, waiting for bands to loosen,
for knots to ease, for the mind to un-grip,
and the natural breath to return,
rerouting ecology, moving life to swamps
and barren places, unlocking quarantined pain,
traveling the topographical map of loss.
The blockage around the heart.
The hibernating dead.
The legs that never stopped wanting
to run.

Lot

The magic trick is not the
death scene with all its
publicity.

It's that who I was died,
that person I was with him,
who believed in love,
and didn't see death
peek through the cracks.

I had to let her go,
see her turn to stone
and crumble, flesh to salt,
nothing when I look back.

In hideous slow-motion
the powder spills out.
I can still hear the sand,
those countless gems,
whisper in the wind.

Under Water

My brother liked tumbling rocks,
microscopes, and Asimov.

I liked puppies, pulling the heads
off barbie dolls, and pretending
to run a grocery store.

We both liked to swim.

We would dive for treasure,
through the silty murk,
and touch the bottom,
causing slow motion
explosions in the sand.

I loved going up and
down in a world
all my own.

He loved the quiet,
how all sound was hushed
by the weight of the water.

At three, he nearly drowned.

He was on the shore
while my mother sat with
me on a blanket.
He put his face down in
the water and stayed there.

I think of our mother
running to him,
wrenching from the
lake and forcing
him to breathe.

O₂

since losing everything

I work to breathe

the muscles of my rib cage
that would lift this mass
of bones

are lax

the work is strenuous
and requiring of focus

I must rally them
to get momentum

and load this machine
with enough oxygen
to make optimism

so much oxygen

is required for that

1/25/16

This is what dying looks like,
I thought, then dismissed it.

My husband of twenty
years sat on the couch
wrapped in a woolen blanket.

Just a cold, the doctors said.
Strange to think about dying, but
Jon's eyes had looked like that.
His irises had looked exploded.
It wasn't long for Jon after that.

I walked the dog because life was
normal. When I got back, he asked
me to take him to the hospital. On
the side table sat the half-eaten bowl
of soup I made for him, some broth,
a piece of carrot, one bean.

In the car we didn't speak.
It was like walking the plank.
Already we were on its long beam.
Then they pulled him away in stages,
attached this and that machine.

The words--it's time to say goodbye--
came out as though I'd
memorized it from script.
I recited the line, and it sat
there, like a stone.

"They need to help you to breathe,"

I said, and he understood.
He showed me how to unlock
his phone, a diagonal swipe
followed by

a square in the right corner,
and he closed his eyes.

That's when we were flung
at high speeds,
completely and irrevocably
apart.

cancelled

timelines are cancelled
flights not just delayed
entire roads must be dug up
and houses reassembled
children spun and whirled
across the moon
the earth that was spinning
on its axis, reconsiders

Hannah

The planet of her feelings
Cannot be reached
At this time
Technology is limited to
Orbital views
Ancient spectacle
Drenched in millenniums
Her surface marked by it
Her own atmosphere
Her own hum
Complete completed done
Like the Godly chord they play
When they show heaven or the sun
Coming through the clouds
She was born a prince
We had to change all the pronouns
Because they are limited too
She laments the inconvenience
Of the body
She is a mathematical equation
That needs solving
But everything is already solved
It only needs to be accounted for
She scrolls through the numeric code
Lining and realigning
Bringing of data into
The resonance of music

*

adrift

adrift
on sea
no direction
only the wake
the pushes and pulls
the clang of a bell
it doesn't matter
where we are
we wait
for the day
we can moor
but now
who can see land?
there is only
distance

Notes on the Book of Love

The Book of Love is written before there is love.
The publishers wear raincoats and meet in the rain-
slicked city, the red and yellow and green light
splattering their neon on black streets.
They drink scotch, smoke cigars,
and discuss schedules for release.

When love becomes book, the story closes shut,
seals like a wound. You can't read it then.
It's under construction, being fitted into layouts,
the print, the letterheads, the brass tiles fit into slots,
slugs into linotype.

When you start to see the galleys,
the weight is pleasant in the hands.
Now you're allowed to see the pages.

The book of your life slammed shut,
sending up a dust storm that took years to clear.
Your room of things spasmed inward.
The house fell apart, not in plaster or in paint,
but in lost cohesion.

The writer, who had been so convincing
at illusion, had a sudden loss of interest.
Scribbles are left scattered on the napkins.

The Book of Love is written before there is love.
Business completed, the publishers linger, taking
in the quiet of the late hour.

The season's offerings, the whole of the catalogue,
glisten in their minds as the light refracts in the last
drops of their smoky drinks.

Black Pumps
for my mother

Black leather pumps took her to work,
to auditions, sweat pouring into them
through the gartered stockings.
Her calves shortened; her body listed
forward, the weight crashing down
on her toes, her toes trying to
hold up the world, taking on the
the whole female problem.
There was the constant demand for
her calves to look perky, giving her
that extra something that made men
take her seriously or think of her at all.
It gave its own kind of power.
Any edge would help, and
she wanted to feel beautiful, to
feel the long line of her body on display,
to feel she might be a work of art.
She took the only pedestal available,
the one that elevates from behind.
She wore them every day until she had
to have her toes broken because nothing
else would stop them from gripping.
Uncle Joe, a doctor, white-headed with
a bushy white mustache, cut her feet
out of prison and set them free, like
the prince from Cinderella but in reverse.

kiss

when you kiss me
you look into the cradle of me
i am the baby open-mouthed
my heart drinks from your heart
i look into the cyclops,
the one eye yours becomes
when we get close,
as you kiss me
and all of it
is yes

Dream-orial

I need water and see
my dead husband hooping
with a furry-legged fangirl.
It's a memorial.
Didn't we do this already?
Nothing to do but grieve again.
Usually, he ignores me now
that he's dead: divorces me,
won't talk about anything,
moves to the back of every train
to a place I can't go.
I'm glad I'm wearing
my young body, the polka-dot
miniskirt, my curly hair
down for a once.
"Is it alright," I ask, "that
now you're gone I do nothing
but name birds and mountains?"
"Yes," he says, "but you need water."
Tom Waits, nearby on the grass,
sings a dirge. He's not meant to
be the show, but he stirs tears,
his grumbly voice fixing the
moment into portrait.
Men lie shirtless on
blankets, with nowhere to go.

death toll

the death toll is
on the weather channel,
mentioned after wind speed and air quality

plagues make me think of all
the strange things that can rain down
from the sky

fish sometimes.
locusts. frogs even.
hail clumping together,
snow-like before melting

we could count all the deaths every day
old age, heart attack, cancer of this or that
despair, car accident, war--
and births--count those too.
add and subtract. math and aftermath

wasn't a toll
a gate we drove through?
my dad would throw coins in
a bucket, and then there was
the metallic plunk
happy bell and
the levitating bar,
the reverse knighting,
the open road

can't breathe

i already couldn't breathe—
grief had wrapped its arms around
my chest like a desperate lover
i couldn't get—
those last sips of delicious breath at the top
where the ribs stay suspended
now it's as if my grief
is infectious
as though it's been released
into the atmosphere
they say infected lungs
look like they have shards of glass
in them
something fragile has shattered
and we can't help but take it in

jerk

pre-programmed nervous system
girded in encoded routines buzzes
click, click/buzz/presets in place
reacts, click, in expected responses, click,
to inputs judged to be of a certain nature
--instinctive intelligence deployed--
subject matter concluded
familiar, predicating pre-patterned response
the knee and so forth, jerks
the system now reinforced, kicks
the wiring completes full-circuit relay
insert new message click
undo jerk, no jerk, un-jerk, escape
stop program
replace with chuckle, laugh,
a wobble when not grasping humor
find punchline without system crash
return click click return

Spring Snow

Welcome to the end of the world--

That's what the cherry blossoms said
today as the petals were falling,
splashing in the air,
floating, making
the lightest of landings.

It's always been the end of the world--
the blossoms say.

Trees, having the seasons in them,
practice dying every year,
and trees, having the grave in them,
live half beneath the ground.
Life is not a fall from grace.
It's a passage.

While some cascade
with a meandering quiet,
some crash through
with more weight than anyone
would think possible,
leaving the earth to quake
long afterwards.

wheel

how many twists and turns
are there in this story factory?
...always putting its spin
on things...
blurry with ups and downs
while the dizzy speck of you is hurled

a kindness will stop the thing
will take your hand
make sure you're steady
as you touch the ground
the calloused hand
will reach out

help you with each step across
the uneven metal platform,
the spaces between the grating, the gaps,
all the ways a foot might catch
the attendant has been there all along
and the ride will stop and start again

Handwashing

Maybe it's the constant hand washing,
that ritual of sacred intruding on
a normally secular life; the water is
the Savior, the soap the Holy Ghost,
the bubbles carrying up our prayers,
and the Host the smell that
purifies the insides of the nose.

In these twenty second intervals
the liquid rushes in to save us;
the same water it always was,
of dinosaurs and cave men and single-
celled amoebas and of the sodden
mammals who climbed out to suddenly
feel the sun-to-skin warmth,
that fated first meeting.

There's so much to wash always,
here on dry land, the underwater
world a blurry memory of dark shapes
feeding in the night. Out in the air,
daylight is a knife so sharp it bites.
Then you need the handwashing again.

The blood pulses out and drips its leaky
faucet, leaving blotchy dots in the sink.
Water will nurse and comfort, wash clean,
dispel the iron stink, even soothe the ache
of betrayal. That the blood, once loyal,
plotted its escape, enlisted the knife to
cut it loose, and amidst all throbbing
alarm, is being carried by liquid,
culprit and savior, to freedom.

The handwashing is the act of
putting water back.
Life pours out in every moment,
and even though the skin would block
it, when we pour the water on
our hands, we put some life,
cleaner than we are,
back in.

*

these are my feet

I go into the meadow,
grass grazing my shins,
my bare feet raw.
The grass is cold and
dappled with dew,
the ground's clay drinking
in its morning tea.
Gobs of air gush
in as though I have only
just begun to breathe.
Bubbles press into
my mouth like
champagne.
They punctuate,
reiterate, fill the page.
Colors pop, the
wind pulses, and
I am surrounded.
The poem is there,
and I have seen it.
It takes me back into
its arms hungrily, for
I am lost child, lost love,
and mother/father all in one.
Tears wash my eyes,
a pool overflowing
in my belly because I am
full, full again,
no longer adrift.
These are my feet,
my feet on the earth,
and I know them.

family portrait

The mother doesn't leave the kitchen.
Television floods like sun, then
like moon. Coke bottles stand at attention.
The daughter waits alone for the bus.
The son hides his eyes in Dostoyevsky.
The father, gone, leaves an office chair,
and burn holes in the couch.
The dogs wander off and the
snow wants in.

The Upper Room

You don't want to hear about God in a poem
or maybe you do (even that is controversial)
and maybe you don't even want a poem
(that so often seems to be the case).

You can't eat it, drink it, watch it on a screen.
You can't click on it and have it open up.
It doesn't make the phone vibrate or ring.
It isn't urgent, contagious, or screaming,
needing to be picked up, nursed or have its
diaper changed, put on a ventilator, given an IV.

It doesn't need to be quarantined or washed or
masked or looked at sideways as in
Are you safe?

But if you don't mind hearing about
God in a poem,
I can tell you that today I sensed
that It looked this way and smiled.
It wasn't worried about humans and
our troubles (I'm sorry to say) and even while
It has compassion and a lot of other things
that mean something like that, like love,
It saw life in all its forms
from biggest to smallest blooming--
        all of it was bounty.

Mask

Clouds drape over the mountains,
Muffling their speech. Even the
Weight of atmosphere silences.
The walls quiet random impacts.
Tucked in, we seek recovery
From the daily illness of life.
Hidden, we find the sock and buskin.
The theatrical masks come off.
Behind the laughing one, the sad face is
Frozen, contorted, and hangs off-center.
Nurture, protection, and pretense each
Have sent tendrils that envelop and
Embrace in their usual wistful weaving.
But the greatest veil is the cocoon
In which the future is wrapped, and
Sealed, waiting to be born.

Ashes

When in contact with mortality,
beware the trademark glare that
disassembles you so that your
excess drops away,
like ash from a cigarette.

Ash won't stand up.
Ash won't play.
Ash laughs at you.

It flakes, flies, catches the wind,
blows back in your face,
attaches to your mouth,
and demands that you taste it.

last line of defense

you are my second skin, my rubber glove
i was sick with loss, you fed me love

you are my mask, my fresh O-2
i can't breathe when i'm not with you

suffocate me in your arm and chest
the only place i want to rest

ventilate me, mouth to mouth,
examine me north to south

i will do the same for you
now you and I are stuck like glue

for ever after you're my scene
our lives are bound in quarantine

Menagerie

Old traumas wake me one morning,
tapping gently at the edges of their tiny box.
It's black and metallic and stuffed into the bottom
of the closet. I carry the chest to the backyard. The
object and scene fight, like a coffin on a sunny day.
I pry off the lid, which clatters on the stones,
startling birds. Out climb giraffe and elephant,
their bodies wrinkled from confinement. They
inflate, the air sucked into them because of
their of absolute lack of it. A smell pours out
that is chalky and inert. The giraffe blinks
her chestnut lashes as she soaks in the
lilac-scented air. Even while she's toppling,
she's trying to eat the leaves off branches near
her. She swallows a rock. The elephant is another
matter. Even though he means well, flapping his
giant ears, whipping his donkey-like tail, and
unfurling his snaky trunk, the damage is
already registered by the flowers under his feet.
It's not his fault that the world crushes so easily.
I feed them peanuts, and the sun and air do their
parts. Their emptiness fills up, though the
giraffe is still desperate, and the elephant would
like to crash into a few more things, to feel the
reassurance of the destruction of things that aren't him.
Now if friends stop by or if delivery people glance
in the window, they might see these giant creatures
lounging in the living room, sipping orange wine,
and listening to Coltrane, the brassy sound tickling
the soft fur inside the Giraffe's furry ears.

Yellow

The news of the day is yellow.
Everywhere you look, yellow in the news.
Yellow has landed.
It rests on the water, the mountains,
the trees, your nose, the daffodils.
It's a light yellow, not the fall kind that is
thick and fermented, developed like
straw into gold. This is a brightness,
a new idea barely tried out,
a little jingle you just made up,
some whistling you can barely hear.
The morning was sponge cake, and
afternoon had rippled frosting.
By bedtime it was lollipop.
The world doesn't mean to scare us.
It's bright and bright again,
no matter what trouble we're in.

9 781716 146237